D1265988

I Am Utterly Unique

Celebrating the Strengths of Children
with Asperger Syndrome and High-Functioning Autism

Elaine Marie Larson

Illustrated by Vivian Strand

APC

Autism Asperger Publishing Co.
P.O. Box 23173
Shawnee Mission, Kansas 66283-0173
www.asperger.net

©2006 Autism Asperger Publishing Company
P.O. Box 23173
Shawnee Mission, KS 66283-0173
www.asperger.net

Publisher's Cataloging-in-Publication

Larson, Elaine M.
    I am utterly unique : celebrating the strengths of children with
Asperger syndrome and high-functioning autism / Elaine M. Larson. –
1st ed. – Shawnee Mission, Kan. : Autism Asperger Pub. Co., 2006.

    p. ; cm.

    ISBN-13: 978-1-931282-89-5
    ISBN-10: 1-931282-89-7
    LCCN: 2006921687
    Audience: ages 4-10.
    Summary: This alphabet book gives an understanding of, and helps to celebrate, the unique qualities and attributes of children with Asperger Syndrome.

    1. Asperger's syndrome in children–Juvenile literature. 2. Self-esteem–Juvenile literature. 3. Self-acceptance–Juvenile literature. 4. Alphabet books. I. Title.

RJ506.A9 L37 2006
(E)–dc22
                                        0605

This book is designed in AT Pelican and Avant Garde.

Printed in South Korea.

Dedication

For Sam with love
from Grandma Elaine

Aa

I Am an Animal lover.

Bb

I have
a Busy
Brain.

Cc

I am a Colossal
Collector.

Dd

I am a
Detail
Detective.

Ee

I have
Enormous
Enthusiasm.

Ff

Gg

Hh

I am a
Happy
Helper.

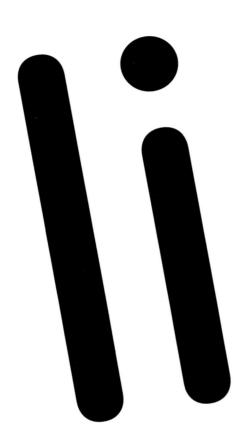

I have an Inventive Imagination.

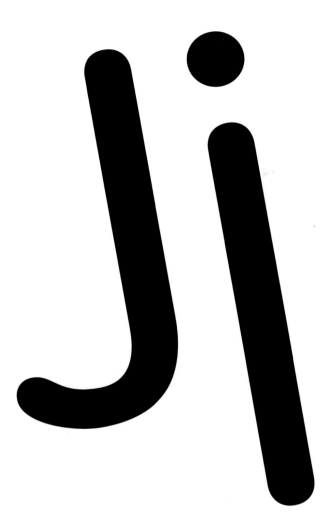

I like
Jumping,
Jogging,
and Jujitsu.

Kk

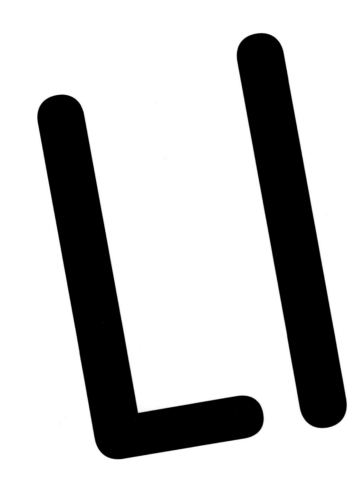

I Like
to
Learn.

Mm

I like
Musical
Motion.

Nn

Oo

I have an
Original
Outlook.

Pp

Qq

Rr

Ss

I am a Smart Student.

Tt

I Tell
the Truth.

Uu

Ww

I live in a Wonderful World.

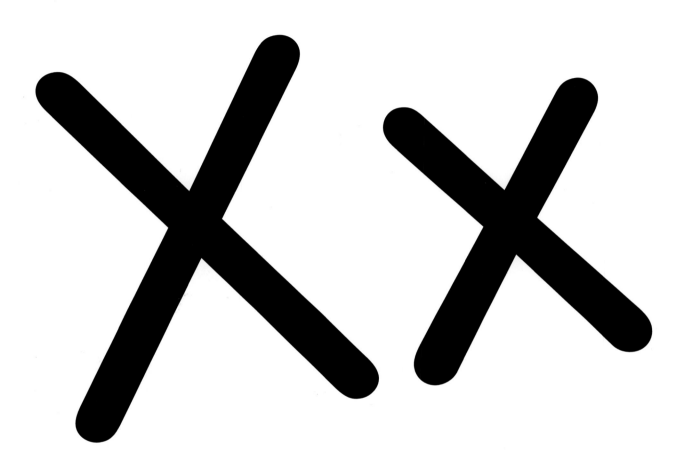

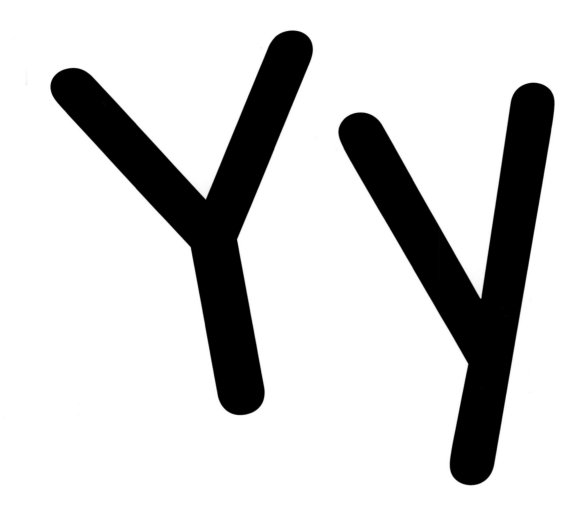

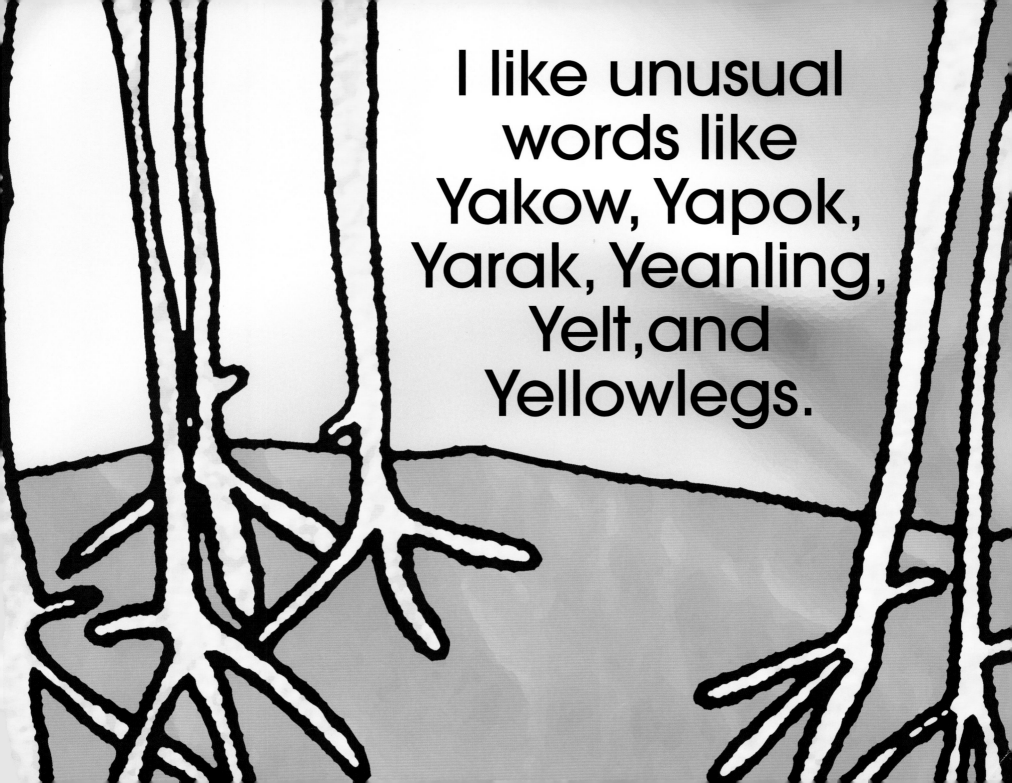

Z z

APC

Autism Asperger Publishing Co.
P.O. Box 23173
Shawnee Mission, Kansas 66283-0173
www.asperger.net